W9-DHW-

Editor
Eric Migliaccio

Editor in Chief
Ina Massler Levin, M.A.

Cover Designer
Karen J. Goldfluss, M.S. Ed.

Cover Artist
Barb Lorseyedi

Creative Director
Karen J. Goldfluss, M.S. Ed.

Imaging
James Edward Grace
Craig Gunnell

CD Application Programmer
Charles Payne

Publisher
Mary D. Smith, M.S. Ed.

Interactive Learning
for All INTERACTIVE WHITEBOARDS Grade 3

TCR 3631

CORRELATED TO COMMON CORE STANDARDS

Paragraph Editing

Pam wanted to win a blue ribbon. she baked cakes, cookies, and cupcakes for the fair. Guess what happened? pam did not win only one blu *blue* ribbon that day. she won three!

★ Developed for ALL Interactive Whiteboards
★ 100 ready-to-edit paragraphs to practice and review grammar, punctuation, and spelling
★ Includes Common Core State Standards

Teacher Created Resources

Teacher Created Resources
6421 Industry Way
Westminster, CA 92683
www.teachercreated.com
ISBN: 978-1-4206-3631-4
© 2013 Teacher Created Resources
Made in U.S.A.

Teacher Created Resources

Table of Contents

Introduction

Imagine a classroom tool that could make grammar and spelling exciting and engaging for your students. *Paragraph Editing* is a program that has been designed to do all of this and more. Compatible with all interactive whiteboards, *Paragraph Editing* offers the many advantages of touchscreen technology and allows your students to participate in learning like never before.

Each *Paragraph Editing* CD comes loaded with the paragraphs from this book. The paragraphs are divided into 25 units, with new grammar rules incorporated into each of the first 15 units. In this way, grammar, punctuation, and spelling concepts are introduced and then reinforced in a systematic manner, allowing students to practice each concept before learning new ones. The final 10 units of each book and CD offer a cumulative reinforcement of all of the rules and concepts previously learned.

These paragraphs can be accessed and printed from the CD or copied from the book. They can be done as in-class work or assigned as homework. Corrections to these paragraphs can then be made on individual computers or on an interactive whiteboard in front of the class. All it takes is a finger or a special pen, depending on the interactive board you use. You and your students can correct the sentences in these ways:

☞ by writing and drawing directly onto the interactive whiteboard

☞ by grabbing punctuation stamps built into the program and dragging them over the corresponding errors

An array of buttons and menus allows you to do (and undo) every correction quickly and easily and in six custom colors. Best of all, it takes just one quick click of a button for teachers and students to see the correct answers. And, as an added teaching tool, another touch of a button will show students the locations of the paragraph's errors without revealing the actual answers.

In addition to the paragraphs included on the CD, the *Paragraph Editing* program allows you to create and save thousands of custom paragraphs. The program can even make incorrect versions of your custom creations by adding errors for you. Teachers can use this tool to tap into their class's creativity with student-generated paragraphs and peer-editing exercises.

Common Core State Standards

The activities in this book meet one or more of the following Common Core State Standards. (© Copyright 2010. National Governors Association Center for Best Practices and Council of Chief State School Officers. All rights reserved.) For more information about the Common Core State Standards, go to *http://www.corestandards.org/*.

Reading Standards: Foundational Skills
Fluency

Standard 1: RF.3.4. Demonstrate understanding of the organization and basic features of print.

- RF.3.4a: Read grade-level text with purpose and understanding.
- RF.3.4c: Use context to confirm or self-correct word recognition and understanding, rereading as necessary.

Language Standards
Conventions of Standard English

Standard 1: L.3.1 Demonstrate command of the conventions of standard English grammar and usage when writing or speaking.

- L.3.1b: Form and use regular and irregular plural nouns.
- L.3.1d: Form and use regular and irregular verbs.
- L.3.1e: Form and use the simple (e.g., *I walked; I walk; I will walk*) verb tenses.
- L.3.1f: Ensure subject-verb and pronoun-antecedent agreement.
- L.3.1h: Use coordinating and subordinating conjunctions.
- L.3.1i: Produce simple, compound, and complex sentences.

Standard 2: L.3.2 Demonstrate command of the conventions of standard English capitalization, punctuation, and spelling when writing.

- L.3.2a: Capitalize appropriate words in titles.
- L.3.2b: Use commas in addresses.
- L.3.2c: Use commas and quotation marks in dialogue.
- L.3.2d: Form and use possessives.
- L.3.2e: Use conventional spelling for high-frequency and other studied words and for adding suffixes to base words (e.g., *sitting, smiled, cries, happiness*).
- L.3.2f: Use spelling patterns and generalizations (e.g., *word families, position-based spellings, syllable patterns, ending rules, meaningful word parts*) in writing words

About the CD

The real flexibility and interactivity of the *Paragraph Editing* program shine through in the resources included on the CD.

☞ Install the CD

Just pop the CD that accompanies this book into your PC or Mac, and you and your students can begin editing paragraphs at individual computers or on the interactive whiteboard in your classroom.

> **Quick Tip:** Step-by-step installation instructions and some troubleshooting tips are provided in the "ReadMe" file on the CD.

☞ The Main Menu

Once you have installed the CD, the Main Menu will appear on your computer screen or interactive whiteboard.

> **Quick Tip:** The Main Menu will open up in full-screen mode. If you wish to resize the Main Menu screen, hit the ESC button. This will allow you to adjust it as needed.

From the Main Menu, you can access all of the features and resources available in the program. To get a detailed explanation of these features, click on the Guide button. This will take you to the *Paragraph Editing* User's Guide.

☞ The User's Guide

Everything you need to know in order to use and operate the *Paragraph Editing* CD and program can be found in the User's Guide. This is also where you will find a useful one-page handout of the editing symbols used in the program. These marks are available as punctuation stamps on the editing screen for each sentence.

Main Menu Screen

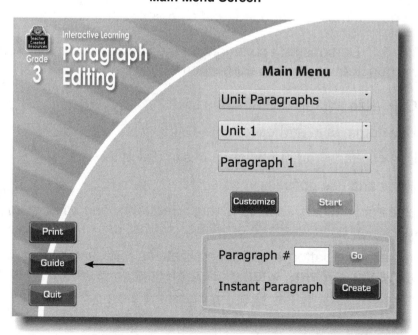

About the CD *(cont.)*

The User's Guide on the CD contains a lot of important and helpful information. However, you may wish to immediately begin editing paragraphs with your students. The following Quick-Start Guide will help you do just that.

Quick-Start Guide for Editing Paragraphs

1. **Launch the Program:** Load the CD and launch the program. If needed, follow the installation instructions given in the "ReadMe" file on the CD.

2. **Click the Start Button:** You can access the **Start** button from the **Main Menu** screen. (See the graphic to the right.) This will take you directly to the editing screen. (See the graphic at the bottom of the page.)

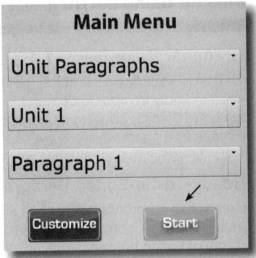

3. **Edit the Paragraph:** Write, draw, or paint directly onto the screen. You may also use the punctuation stamps located on either side of the screen. Grab, drag, and drop these stamps onto, above, or below the word to correct the errors.

4. **Check Your Work:** Click on the **Show Errors** button to give your students hints about where the errors can be found in the paragraph. Click on the **Show Correct** button to reveal the correct version of the paragraph.

5. **Edit a New Paragraph:** Click on the **Next** button to continue the editing lesson with a new paragraph.

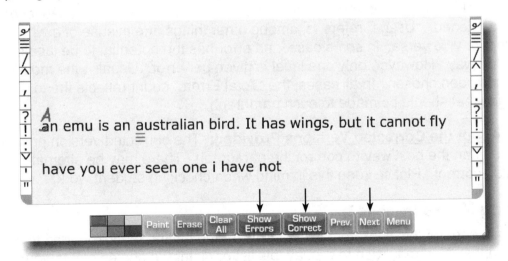

About the Book

There are two main components to the *Paragraph Editing* program: a book and a CD. These two parts were designed to be complementary, but they can also be used independently of one another. This 112-page book contains the following features:

☞ **Common Core State Standards** (page 3)

The grammar rules and concepts reviewed in this book meet Common Core State Standards for grade-level appropriateness.

☞ **Tips for Using the CD** (pages 4–5)

These two pages include tips for getting started with the CD that accompanies this book.

☞ **Grammar Rules** (pages 7–11)

This book includes a list of the punctuation, capitalization, and usage rules students will need to know in order to correct the paragraphs. New rules are introduced in each of the first 15 units, allowing students to learn increasingly difficult grammar concepts at a measured pace, while reviewing the ones they have previously learned. The final 10 units serve as a cumulative review of the rules learned in the first 15 units.

☞ **Ready-To-Be-Edited Paragraphs** (pages 12–111)

On each even-numbered page of this section, there are two error-filled paragraphs. (In all, this book contains a total of 100 unique paragraphs.) These paragraphs contain plenty of space between lines so students may add editing marks and rewrite incorrectly spelled words. Copy these pages for use as in-class assignments or send them home as homework.

On the odd-numbered pages that follow, the corrected versions of the paragraphs are given. The revisions are shown in gray, and a summary of the errors that can be found in each paragraph is provided.

Note About the Summary of Errors: The terms used in this list are meant to help you quickly locate specific types of errors. Many terms refer to both the omission and the misuse of that element. *Examples:* The term "Periods" is given when a period is missing and also when one is used incorrectly (in place of a question mark, for example). "Capitalization" is a broad term used to refer to any instance where a capital or lowercase letter is needed. "Usage" refers to, among other things, the misuse of *a* when *an* is needed, or vice versa. In some cases, an error has the potential to be labeled in more than one way. However, only one label is given per error. Usually, the most specific term has been chosen. In all cases, the "Total Errors" count reflects the total number of changes that should be made to each paragraph.

Note About the Corrected Versions Provided: The corrected version provided shows what is often the best way to correct the paragraph. There may be alternate ways that are also correct. Please keep this in mind when checking student work.

☞ **Editing Marks** (page 112)

The final page of this book contains a full list of the editing marks needed to correct the paragraphs. You may wish to display this list or distribute copies of it to your students.

Grammar Rules

The following pages include most of the grammar, usage, and punctuation rules students will need to know to edit the paragraphs in this book. The units in which these rules are applicable are listed in parentheses after each rule.

Rule 1: A *sentence* is a group of words that tells a complete thought. Capitalize the first word in a sentence. A *statement* is a sentence that tells something. Put a period at the end of a telling sentence. A *question* is a sentence that asks something. Put a question mark at the end of an asking sentence. An *exclamation* is a sentence that shows strong feeling. It ends with an exclamation mark. A *command* is a sentence that tells someone to do something. It ends with a period or an exclamation mark. (**Units 1–30**)

- **My dog is black.**
- **Do you have a pet?**
- **Please print your name.**
- **Get out of the street!**

Rule 2: Capitalize the word *I*. (**Units 1–30**)

- **Scott and I are friends.**

Rule 3: *Proper nouns* name specific people, places, and things. A proper noun begins with a capital letter. *Common nouns* are not specific. A common noun does not begin with a capital letter. (**Units 1–30**)

- **That dog is named Max.** (common noun = *dog*; proper noun = *Max*)

Rule 4: An *abbreviation* is a short form of a word. Capitalize name titles and put a period after ones that have been shortened into an abbreviation. Also capitalize and put a period after initials, which are letters used instead of a full name. Do not capitalize *a.m.* or *p.m.* (**Units 1–30**)

- **The building is owned by Mr. Payne and Dr. Anna Lee.**
- **The author of the book is J.P. Wilson.**
- **School starts at 7:00 a.m.**

Rule 5: Capitalize the days of the week, months of the year, and holidays. Do not capitalize seasons of the year. (**Units 1–30**)

- **My favorite season is spring.**
- **Is Memorial Day on a Monday in May?**

Rule 6: A *run-on sentence* has two complete thoughts that run into each other. Use a period or other end punctuation to divide these thoughts into two sentences. (**Units 1–30**)

- **I woke up late my alarm clock is broken.** (*incorrect*)
- **I woke up late. My alarm clock is broken.** (*correct*)

Rule 7: A *colon* is used between the hour and minutes when writing the time of day. (**Units 1–30**)

- **We went to school at 8:00.**

Grammar Rules *(cont.)*

Rule 8: Use a comma to separate the day and year or to separate the day and month. Use a comma to separate a city and state or country. When these elements appear in the beginning or middle of a sentence, use a comma to separate them from the rest of the sentence. **(Units 2–30)**

- **She was born on Thursday, November 2, 2006.**
- **Andrea flew from Houston, Texas, to Paris, France.**
- **July 7, 2007, was the day we met.**

Rule 9: A series is a list of three or more items. Use a comma to separate three or more words or groups of words in a series. **(Units 2–30)**

- **Would you rather have pizza, pasta, or a hamburger?**
- **We went to the beach, ate lunch, and saw a movie on Saturday.**

Rule 10: A *singular noun* names one person, place, thing, or idea. A *plural noun* names more than one person, place, thing, or idea. Add *s* to most nouns to make them plural. Add *es* to words that end in *s, ch, sh, x,* and *z.* **(Units 3–30)**

- **I have two small <u>dogs</u> and one big <u>dog</u>.**
- **I see one blue <u>dish</u> and two red <u>dishes</u>.**

Rule 11: Use *a* or *an* before singular nouns. Use *a* before words that begin with a consonant sound. Use *an* before words that begin with a vowel or vowel sound. **(Units 3–30)**

- **He ate <u>a</u> piece of toast and <u>an</u> egg <u>an</u> hour before school began.**

Rule 12: Nouns that end in the letter *y* have special rules for making plurals. If the word ends with a vowel followed by *y,* just add *s.* If the word ends with a consonant followed by *y,* change the *y* to *i* and add *es.* **(Units 4–30)**

- **Dad put his <u>keys</u> in his coat pocket.**
- **I went to three birthday <u>parties</u> in June.**

Rule 13: Nouns that end in *f* or *fe* also have a special rule for making plurals. In most words, change the *f* to *v* and add *es.* **(Units 4–30)**

- **I found six butter <u>knives</u> and one bread <u>knife</u> in the drawer.**
- **One <u>calf</u> has black spots. Two <u>calves</u> have brown spots.**

Rule 14: A *possessive noun* shows ownership. Use an *apostrophe* and an *s* (*'s*) after a noun to show that something belongs to one person, group, or thing. To form the plural possessive of a plural noun that ends in *s,* add only an apostrophe. If the plural noun does not end in *s,* add an apostrophe and an *s.* **(Units 5–30)**

- **<u>Beth's</u> guitar is sitting next to <u>Jess's</u> drum set.**
- **Both of his <u>brothers'</u> bikes are blue.**
- **We visited the <u>children's</u> library yesterday.**

Grammar Rules *(cont.)*

Rule 15: A pronoun is a word that is used in place of a noun. Use the pronouns *I* and *me* correctly. Use the pronoun *I* when you are doing something. Use the pronoun *me* when something happens to you. **(Units 6–30)**

- **Mom and <u>I</u> went to Hawaii.**
- **She waved to Bob and <u>me</u>.**

Rule 16: Use the personal pronouns *we/us, she/he, her/him,* and *they/them* correctly. Also use possessive pronouns (e.g., *mine, ours, his, hers, its, theirs*) correctly. **(Units 6–30)**

Use "we" when you and others are doing something.

Use "she/he/they" when a person or group is doing something.

Use "us" when something happens to you and others.

Use "her/him/them" when something is happening to a person or a group.

- **<u>We</u> went to school.**
- **<u>He</u> is riding the bike.**
- **Sam gave <u>him</u> a ride.**
- **That house is <u>ours</u>.**

- **<u>They</u> gave the trophy to <u>us</u>.**
- **<u>She</u> will cook dinner for <u>them</u>.**
- **Bill took <u>her</u> to the movie.**
- **Is this book <u>yours</u>?**

Rule 17: A *contraction* is a word made by joining two words. When joining the words, a letter or letters are left out. An apostrophe is put in the word at the spot where the letter or letters are missing. **(Units 7–30)**

- **<u>We are</u> going home.**
- **She <u>did not</u> see him.**
- **He <u>will</u> be there soon.**

<u>We're</u> going home.

She <u>didn't</u> see him.

<u>He'll</u> be there soon.

Rule 18: A name can be made into a contraction or a possessive by adding *'s*. The *'s* can mean "is" or "has," depending on the sentence. **(Units 7–30)**

- **<u>Mary's</u> going to Canada this summer.** *(contraction for "is")*
- **<u>Mary's</u> been packing for her trip.** *(contraction for "has")*
- **I saw <u>Mary's</u> car parked in the lot.** *(possessive)*

Rule 19: The verb often shows the action of the sentence. When the subject of the sentence is singular, an *s* or *es* is usually added to the verb (except with the pronouns *I* or *you*.) When the subject is plural, an *s* is not added to the verb. **(Units 8–30)**

- **Ryan <u>eats</u> a lot of food. Eric and Bob <u>eat</u> more food.**
- **You <u>eat</u> broccoli for lunch. I do not <u>eat</u> broccoli.**
- **The school <u>fixes</u> lunch for us. They <u>fix</u> lunch for us every day.**

Grammar Rules *(cont.)*

Rule 20: The verbs *am, are, is, was,* and *were* are forms of the word *be*. They are not action words. Instead, they tell what someone or something is like. **(Units 8–30)**

Use "am" with the word "I."

Use "is" and "are" when talking about what is happening now.

Use "was" and "were" when talking about things that have already happened.

Use "is" and "was" when talking about one person, place, thing, or idea.

Use "are" and "were" when talking about more than one person, place, thing, or idea, and with the word "you."

- I <u>am</u> six years old. You <u>are</u> older than I am.
- Jim <u>is</u> seven years old. Last year, Jim <u>was</u> six.
- Kate and Nate <u>are</u> eight. They <u>were</u> seven last year.

Rule 21: A *present-tense verb* shows action that happens now. A *past-tense verb* tells about an action that already happened. Add *ed* to most verbs to form the past tense. In addition to *s* and *es*, the ending *ing* can also be added to present-tense verbs. If the verb has a single vowel and ends with a consonant, the last consonant is usually doubled before adding *ed* or *ing*. If the word ends with a silent *e*, drop the final *e* before adding *ed* or *ing*. **(Units 8–30)**

- The car <u>stops</u> here now. It also <u>stopped</u> here yesterday. Will it be <u>stopping</u> here every day?
- I <u>wave</u> goodbye. I <u>waved</u> to everybody. I am <u>waving</u> my hand.

Rule 22: If a verb ends with a consonant and *y*, change the *y* to *i* and add *es* to form the present-tense verb. If a verb ends with a consonant and *y*, change the *y* to *i* and add *ed* to form a past-tense verb. **(Units 9–30)**

- Each team <u>tries</u> to win.
- I <u>tried</u> to hit a home run.

Rule 23: The past tense of some verbs is made by changing the spelling. **(Units 9–30)**

- Last week my dog <u>ran</u> away. *(run)*
- He <u>bought</u> some milk at the store. *(buy)*
- He <u>drew</u> a picture in art class. *(draw)*

Rule 24: Helping verbs are sometimes used with main action verbs. Some examples of helping verbs are *has, have, had, is, are, was, were,* and *will*. **(Units 9–30)**

- Yesterday I saw you at the mall. I <u>have seen</u> you there before.
- We <u>were</u> eating dinner when you called.

Grammar Rules _(cont.)_

Rule 25: A _quotation_ shows a speaker's exact words. Use _quotation marks_ at the beginning and ending of a quotation to show where the speaker started and stopped talking. Begin a quotation with a capital letter. In a _telling_ sentence, use a comma between the quotation and the rest of the sentence. **(Units 10–30)**

- Sal said, "We are going to the zoo."
- "We are going to the zoo," said Sal.

Rule 26: In an _asking_ sentence, use a question mark at the end of the quotation. If the quotation is before the speaker's name, put a period at the end of the sentence. If the speaker's name is before the quotation, separate the quotation with a comma. The same rules apply in an _exclamation_. **(Units 10–30)**

- Lily asked, "Can I go with you?"
- "Can I go with you?" asked Lily.
- "That house is on fire!" shouted Al.
- Al shouted, "That house is on fire!"

Rule 27: When writing the title of a book, movie, play, newspaper, music collection, or television show, underline (or italicize) the entire title and capitalize the first word, the last word, and each important word. Follow the same capitalization rules, but use quotation marks around the titles of stories, poems, and songs. **(Units 12–30)**

- We read the book <u>Holes</u> in class.
- We listened to "Somewhere Over the Rainbow" from <u>The Wizard of Oz</u>.

Rule 28: A _homophone_ is a word that sounds the same as another word but has a different spelling and/or meaning. Be careful not to confuse these and other misused words, such as _are/our_ and _it's/its_. **(Units 13–30)**

- I can <u>see</u> the ship out on the <u>sea</u>.
- <u>Are</u> you coming to <u>our</u> house today?
- <u>It's</u> time to give the dog <u>its</u> bath.

Rule 29: If two complete thoughts are joined by a conjunction (e.g., _and, but, so, yet_) to create one sentence, put a comma before the conjunction. **(Units 14–25)**

- I'm going to bake cookies, and you should help me eat them.
- Pablo wanted to play ball, but he couldn't find the field.

Rule 30: A _negative_ is a word like _no, not, none,_ or _never_. A contraction with the word _not_ is also a negative. Do not use two negatives together in a sentence. **(Units 15–30)**

- She never had ~~no~~ lunch. She never had <u>any</u> lunch.
- Can't you see ~~nothing~~? Can't you see <u>anything</u>?

~~~~~~

an emu is an australian bird. It has wings, but it cannot fly have you ever seen one i have not

~~~~~~

Rick and ella live on a farm. Their school day starts at 730 a m they wake up at 600 to feed the hens do you think that is too urly

an emu is an australian bird. It has wings, but it cannot fly. have you ever seen one? i have not.

**Unit 1 • Paragraph 1
Errors**

Capitalization 4
Periods 2
Question
 Marks 1

Total Errors: 7

Rick and ella live on a farm. Their school day starts at 7:30 a.m. they wake up at 6:00 to feed the hens. do you think that is too ~~urly~~ early?

**Unit 1 • Paragraph 2
Errors**

Capitalization 3
Colons 2
Periods 3
Question
 Marks 1
Spelling 1

Total Errors: 10

~~~~~~

Miles and robin wanted to play baseball at Oak st park. Their mother said they could go after they finished their chores they had to clean their rooms and mopp the kitchen floor. They did their chores and got to the park in less than an hour

~~~~~~

Booker T Washington was born a slave in the state of virginia in 1856 that was a few years before the Civil War was fought and slaves were declared freee. Booker later started a school called tuskegee institute. He helped others gain equality through education

Miles and robin wanted to play baseball at Oak st park. Their mother said they could go after they finished their chores they had to clean their rooms and mopp the kitchen floor. They did their chores and got to the park in less than an hour

Unit 1 • Paragraph 3 Errors

Capitalization 4
Periods 3
Spelling 1

Total Errors: 8

Booker T Washington was born a slave in the state of virginia in 1856 that was a few years before the Civil War was fought and slaves were declared freee. Booker later started a school called tuskegee institute. He helped others gain equality through education

Unit 1 • Paragraph 4 Errors

Capitalization 4
Periods 3
Spelling 1

Total Errors: 8

~~~~~~~~~~~~~~~~~~~~~~~~~~~~~~~~~~~

Pam wanted to win a blue ribbon she baked cakes cookies and cupcakes for the fair. Guess what happened pam did not win only one blu ribbon that day. She won three!

~~~~~~~~~~~~~~~~~~~~~~~~~~~~~~~~~~~

My family and i have been to a lot of places. We visited the Smoky Mountains in virginia last winter. We flew out to Oregon in the spring. We even drove across the Golden gate Bridge in san francisco california that was amazing

Pam wanted to win a blue ribbon. she baked cakes, cookies, and cupcakes for the fair. Guess what happened? pam did not win only one blue ribbon that day. She won three!

Unit 2 • Paragraph 5 Errors

Capitalization 2
Commas. 2
Periods. 1
Question
Marks. 1
Spelling 1

Total Errors: 7

My family and i have been to a lot of places. We visited the Smoky Mountains in virginia last winter. We flew out to Oregon in the spring. We even drove across the Golden gate Bridge in san francisco, california. that was amazing!

Unit 2 • Paragraph 6 Errors

Capitalization 7
Commas. 1
Exclamation
Points. 1
Periods. 1

Total Errors: 10

I love going to the circus. that is why i was so excited when a circus came to Silver Creek nebraska, on may 6 2012. I was able to see the performance on opening night what an incredible show. I saw clowns acrobats and a giant elephant named tiny.

The Arctic is one of the coldest regions on earth. Would it surprise you to learn that manny diferent animals live there. Reindeer and caribou roam the arctic in large herds bears foxes and hares also live there

I love going to the circus. that is why i was so excited when a circus came to Silver Creek nebraska, on may 6, 2012. I was able to see the performance on opening night what an incredible show! I saw clowns acrobats and a giant elephant named tiny.

Unit 2 • Paragraph 7 Errors

Capitalization 6
Commas....... 4
Exclamation
  Points........ 1
Periods........ 1

Total Errors: 12

The Arctic is one of the coldest regions on earth. Would it surprise you to learn that manny (many) diferent (different) animals live there. Reindeer and caribou roam the arctic in large herds bears foxes and hares also live there.

Unit 2 • Paragraph 8 Errors

Capitalization 3
Commas....... 2
Periods........ 2
Question
  Marks........ 1
Spelling 2

Total Errors: 10

Maria Blum has always wanted to be a veterinarian. She enjoyed a lecture given by dr frank smith he visited her class on Tuesday and talked about performing Surgery on small animal. Dr. Smith has worked at the springville veterinary Hospital on Arthur st for the last forteen year.

my day begins at 700 each morning. I shower, get dressed, and eat breakfast i yoosually have a bowl of cereal, two piece of toast, and a egg. Then I am off to catch the school buss it picks me up near the corner of canary ave and lemon St.

Maria Blum has always wanted to be a veterinarian. She enjoyed a lecture given by dr frank smith he visited her class on Tuesday and talked about performing Surgery on small animal.

Dr. Smith has worked at the springville veterinary Hospital on Arthur st for the last forteen year.

fourteen

**Unit 3 • Paragraph 9
Errors**

Capitalization	8
Periods	3
Plurals	2
Spelling	1

Total Errors: 14

my day begins at 700 each morning. I shower, get dressed, and eat breakfast i yoosually have a bowl of cereal, two piece of toast, and a egg.

usually

an

Then I am off to catch the school buss it picks me up near the corner of canary ave and lemon St.

**Unit 3 • Paragraph 10
Errors**

Capitalization	6
Colons	1
Periods	3
Plurals	1
Spelling	2
Usage	1

Total Errors: 14

Something was in the closet. It was scratching at the door jake looked at the clock. The time was 1159 at night. Jake reached for an flashlight and slowly opened the closet dor out jumped Mr Whiskers. jake breathed a sigh of relief and petted his cat

Disneyland is a amusement park designed by Walt disney it opened in anaheim california, on July 17 1955. Now there are Disney parks in such place as florida france and japan.

Something was in the closet. It was scratching

at the door. jake looked at the clock. The time

was 11:59 at night. Jake reached for ~~an~~ *a* flashlight

and slowly opened the closet ~~dor~~ *door*. out jumped

Mr. Whiskers. jake breathed a sigh of relief and

petted his cat.

Unit 3 • Paragraph 11 Errors

Capitalization 3
Colons 1
Periods 4
Spelling 1
Usage 1

Total Errors: 10

Disneyland is ~~a~~ *an* amusement park designed by

Walt disney. it opened in anaheim, california, on

July 17, 1955. Now there are Disney parks in

such place*s* as florida, france, and japan.

Unit 3 • Paragraph 12 Errors

Capitalization 7
Commas 4
Periods 1
Plurals 1
Usage 1

Total Errors: 14

Name: _____   Date: _____

~~~~~~

mindy, Mark and i visited the san diego zoo

last monday. We were lucky enough to see a few

penguin egg hatch. I was right neer the exhibit

when the babys were born it was so exciting?

~~~~~~

C j and juan passed out spoons knifes and

plastic tubs sam and i poured the cream. Mrs.

banks told us to attach the lids and shake the

tubs hard. In a few minute, each of us had a

lump of buttter we spread it on crackers and

had a tasty snack.

mindy, Mark and i visited the san diego zoo last monday. We were lucky enough to see a few penguin egg[s] hatch. I was right near the exhibit when the babys[babies] were born it was so exciting?[!]

Unit 4 • Paragraph 13 Errors

Capitalization 7
Commas 1
Exclamation
  Points......... 1
Periods......... 1
Plurals 2
Spelling 1

Total Errors: 13

C j and juan passed out spoons, knifes[knives] and plastic tubs, sam and i poured the cream. Mrs. banks told us to attach the lids and shake the tubs hard. In a few minute[s], each of us had a lump of buttter[butter] we spread it on crackers and had a tasty snack.

Unit 4 • Paragraph 14 Errors

Capitalization 6
Commas 2
Periods......... 4
Plurals 2
Spelling 1

Total Errors: 15

~~~~~~

A continent is a big piece of land. There are seven continents on our planet their name are North america, south America, europe africa asia australia, and Antarctica. Africa has the most countrys, but asia is home to the most people

~~~~~~

my garden put on a awesome show this Spring the roses were blooms of gold dark red and white. The pansys provided a purple presence. Around these other flower were the pale yellow orange and pink poppys i had planted

A continent is a big piece of land. There are seven continents on our planet. their names are North america, south America, europe, africa, asia, australia, and Antarctica. Africa has the most

countries
countrys, but asia is home to the most people.

Unit 4 • Paragraph 15 Errors

Capitalization 8
Commas 3
Periods 2
Plurals 2

Total Errors: 15

an
my garden put on a awesome show this Spring.

the roses were blooms of gold, dark red, and white.

pansies
The pansys provided a purple presence. Around

s
these other flower were the pale yellow, orange,

poppies
and pink poppys i had planted.

Unit 4 • Paragraph 16 Errors

Capitalization 4
Commas 4
Periods 2
Plurals 3
Usage 1

Total Errors: 14

Name: _____   Date: _____

~~~~~~

Cowboys use their hats in many way. Hats are used to shade a cowboys eyes and to protect him from the sun the hat also protects the cowboys head from tree branchs thorny shrubs and even the weather a hat can be used like a umbrella when it rains.

~~~~~~

Grandpas house is by a creek in the woods he often sees deers rabbits and foxs run across the creek. A giant squirrel once crawled through a open window to fetch a acorn That nearly scared the fur off of grandpas cat!

Cowboys use their hats in many way. Hats are used to shade a cowboys eyes and to protect him from the sun the hat also protects the cowboys head from tree branchs thorny shrubs and even the weather a hat can be used like a umbrella when it rains.

Unit 5 • Paragraph 17
Errors

Apostrophes	2
Capitalization	2
Commas	2
Periods.	2
Plurals	2
Usage	1

Total Errors: 11

Grandpas house is by a creek in the woods he often sees deers rabbits and foxs run across the creek. A giant squirrel once crawled through a open window to fetch a acorn That nearly scared the fur off of grandpas cat!

Unit 5 • Paragraph 18
Errors

Apostrophes	2
Capitalization	2
Commas	2
Periods.	2
Plurals	2
Usage	2

Total Errors: 12

Wally Worm woke up stretched, and started on a early search for food he met up with three of his friend along the way. They had come up with an idea. His friends idea was to look under the apple trees in mr. thomas yard wally agreed that it was a good plan.

Sallys sisters name is polly Jean, but everyone calls her p j. Their family is going to Disney World in orlando florida, on august 21 the two sister are counting the days until they can go. There are 114 day left until the big trip

Wally Worm woke up, stretched, and started on
an
a early search for food, he met up with three of

his friends along the way. They had come up with

an idea. His friends' idea was to look under the

apple trees in mr. thomas's yard, wally agreed that

it was a good plan.

Unit 5 • Paragraph 19 Errors

Apostrophes 2
Capitalization 4
Commas 1
Periods 2
Plurals 1
Usage 1

Total Errors: 11

Sally's sisters' name is polly Jean, but everyone

calls her p. j. Their family is going to Disney World

in orlando, florida, on august 21, the two sisters

are counting the days until they can go. There

are 114 days left until the big trip.

Unit 5 • Paragraph 20 Errors

Apostrophes 2
Capitalization 7
Commas 1
Periods 3
Plurals 2

Total Errors: 15

Name: _____ Date: _____

Amy and me enjoy being in our school band it is a place where us can meet many different people who share our musical interests. We even got to march in a parade on St patricks Day this year what a enjoyable experience

Mr and Mrs Perezs baby was born on Thursday september 30 they have named him Pedro Perez, Jr there will be a party on saturday october 9 to welcome little pedro into our lifes. The address is 329 flower blvd

Amy and me [I] enjoy being in our school band. it is a place where us [we] can meet many different people who share our musical interests. We even got to march in a parade on St. patricks Day this year. what an enjoyable experience!

Unit 6 • Paragraph 21 Errors

Apostrophes..... 1
Capitalization 3
Exclamation
 Points......... 1
Periods 3
Pronouns 2
Usage......... 1

Total Errors: 11

Mr. and Mrs. Perezs baby was born on Thursday. september 30. they have named him Pedro Perez, Jr. there will be a party on saturday. october 9. to welcome little pedro into our lifes [lives]. The address is 329 flower blvd.

Unit 6 • Paragraph 22 Errors

Apostrophes..... 1
Capitalization 8
Commas........ 3
Periods......... 5
Plurals 1

Total Errors: 18

Name: _____ Date: _____

Eve and me had a amazing time visiting a museum in chicago Illinois. we made a huge dinosaur move by pushing a red button. Eve also turned a big wheel to create static electricity everyone laughed when eves long hair stood straight up on her hedd

The twins have a morning routine. ken brushes his tooths while keith combs his hair. Then them put on the clothes that their mother has laid out for they. Both Brothers lunchs are packed and ready to go by the time they run downstairs they are out the door by 745.

Eve and ~~me~~ (I) had ~~a~~ (an) amazing time visiting a museum in chicago, Illinois. we made a huge dinosaur move by pushing a red button. Eve also turned a big wheel to create static electricity. everyone laughed when eves long hair stood straight up on her ~~hedd~~ (head)!

Unit 6 • Paragraph 23 Errors

Apostrophes	1
Capitalization	4
Commas	1
Exclamation Points	1
Periods	1
Pronouns	1
Spelling	1
Usage	1

Total Errors: 11

The twins have a morning routine. ken brushes his ~~tooths~~ (teeth) while keith combs his hair. Then ~~them~~ (they) put on the clothes that their mother has laid out for ~~they~~ (them). Both Brothers lunchs are packed and ready to go by the time they run downstairs. they are out the door by 745.

Unit 6 • Paragraph 24 Errors

Apostrophes	1
Capitalization	4
Colons	1
Periods	1
Plurals	2
Pronouns	2

Total Errors: 11

Little william had always dreamed of the day

when hed be able to command a spaceship. He

was 28 year old when he led the first manned

mission to the planet mars his crew calls him

Capt w r nichols. They tell him that hes the best

commander in the universe.

The train hadnt arrived by 845. This made

Marty xtremely nervous martys boss wouldnt accept

any excuses. the train finally arrived at 905 Marty

breathed a sigh of relief picked up his briefcase,

and prepared to board the train

Little william had always dreamed of the day when he'd be able to command a spaceship. He was 28 years old when he led the first manned mission to the planet mars. his crew calls him Capt. w. r. nichols. They tell him that he's the best commander in the universe.

Unit 7 • Paragraph 25 Errors

Apostrophes..... 2
Capitalization 6
Periods 4
Plurals 1

Total Errors: 13

The train hadn't arrived by 8:45. This made Marty extremely nervous. marty's boss wouldn't accept any excuses. the train finally arrived at 9:05. Marty breathed a sigh of relief, picked up his briefcase, and prepared to board the train.

Unit 7 • Paragraph 26 Errors

Apostrophes..... 3
Capitalization 2
Colons 2
Commas........ 1
Periods 3
Spelling 1

Total Errors: 12

Anns class is taking a field trip to the

Willamette River in portland oregon in march. Dr

roberts will ask ann and her classmates to study

the birds and plant that live along the river. Anns

especially excited to learn about the canadian

gooses that live there.

The Ross Familys summer vacation took place

at Sunshine St Beach. The rosses spent a week

there. Rita loved the water Shes a excellent

swimmer. Rex collected shellls hes ritas

younger brother. Mr and mrs Ross just

relaxed and read books.

Ann's class is taking a field trip to the

Willamette River in portland, oregon, in march. Dr.

roberts will ask ann and her classmates to study

the birds and plant^s that live along the river. Ann's

especially excited to learn about the canadian

geese
gooses that live there.

**Unit 7 • Paragraph 27
Errors**

Apostrophes 2
Capitalization 6
Commas 2
Periods 1
Plurals 2

Total Errors: 13

The Ross Family's summer vacation took place

at Sunshine St. Beach. The rosses spent a week

there. Rita loved the water. She's *an* a excellent

shells
swimmer. Rex collected shellls he's rita's

younger brother. Mr. and mrs. Ross just

relaxed and read books.

**Unit 7 • Paragraph 28
Errors**

Apostrophes 4
Capitalization 4
Periods 5
Spelling 1
Usage 1

Total Errors: 15

All three of the jordan brothers work at the garage. Joe fixs engines john repairs dents and jimmy paint the cars. The jordans business are very successful. Everyone say theyre honest and do goode work

the three friend went campping and had a great time. danny pitchd the tent after carl made sure they was not disturbing any animals home. Larry laid out the supplys while carl gatherd firewood The teamwork between the three friends made the trip a success

All three of the jordan brothers work at the garage. Joe fixs engines john repairs dents, and jimmy paint the cars. The jordans' business are very successful. Everyone say theyre honest and do goode work.

Unit 8 • Paragraph 29 Errors

Apostrophes 2
Capitalization 4
Commas 2
Periods 1
Spelling 1
Verbs 4

Total Errors: 14

the three friend went campping and had a great time. danny pitchd the tent after carl made sure they was not disturbing any animals home. Larry laid out the supplys while carl gatherd firewood. The teamwork between the three friends made the trip a success.

Unit 8 • Paragraph 30 Errors

Apostrophes 1
Capitalization 4
Periods 2
Plurals 2
Spelling 1
Verbs 3

Total Errors: 13

Sam dad and me worked for three hour in the garden today. We plantted eggplant squash and cucumbers. We're planting peppers tomorrow. Dad is hopeing our garden will be thriving by mothers day in may

Unit 8
Paragraph
31

There are many thing to see and do at the fair. You can see ladys dresssed as fairys and pigs playing in their pens. You can eats delicious berry pies and fresh corn on the cob its wonderful to see so many person haveing fun!

Unit 8
Paragraph
32

Unit 8 • Paragraph 31

Sam, dad, and me [I] worked for three hour [hours] in the garden today. We plantted [planted] eggplant, squash, and cucumbers. We're planting peppers tomorrow. Dad is hopeing [hoping] our garden will be thriving by mothers [mother's] day in may [May].

**Unit 8 • Paragraph 31
Errors**

Apostrophes. 1
Capitalization 4
Commas. 4
Periods 1
Plurals 1
Pronouns 1
Verbs 2

Total Errors: 14

Unit 8 • Paragraph 32

There are many thing [things] to see and do at the fair. You can see ladys [ladies] dresssed [dressed] as fairys [fairies] and pigs playing in their pens. You can eats [eat] delicious berry pies and fresh corn on the cob, its [It's] wonderful to see so many person [people] haveing [having] fun!

**Unit 8 • Paragraph 32
Errors**

Apostrophes. 1
Capitalization 1
Periods 1
Plurals 4
Spelling 1
Verbs 2

Total Errors: 10

alaska becomed the 49th state on january 3 1959. Its the biggest state in the united states of america. Alaskas land produce such rich natural resource as oil gold and trees would you likes to visit Alaska.

where was peter hiding lisa couldnt found him in any of the place she looked. She thinked about giveing up. Then her seen a pair of shoes sticking out from behind the curtains

alaska becomed [became] the 49th state on january 3,

1959. Its the biggest state in the united states of

america. Alaskas land produce [s] such rich natural

resource [s] as oil, gold, and trees, would you likes [s] to

visit Alaska?

Unit 9 • Paragraph 33 Errors

Apostrophes..... 2
Capitalization 6
Commas........ 3
Periods......... 1
Plurals 1
Question
  Marks........ 1
Verbs 3

Total Errors: 17

where was peter hiding? lisa couldnt found [find] him

in any of the place [s] she looked. She thinked [thought] about

giveing [giving] up. Then her seen [she saw] a pair of shoes sticking

out from behind the curtains.

Unit 9 • Paragraph 34 Errors

Apostrophes..... 1
Capitalization 3
Periods......... 1
Plurals 1
Pronouns 1
Question
  Marks........ 1
Verbs 4

Total Errors: 12

the baby chicks beginned to hatch very slowly

We seen their tiny beaks pokeing through the

cracked shells, and we heared they tiny peeping.

we holded our breaths and watched closely. all

six egg was almost hatched. we knowed itd be so

wonderful to see those babys being born!

Mom and Dad said i could finally have a pet

of my own They taked me to petes Pet Shop to

pick one out. I looked at two fishes three birds

and four mouses. I choosed a mouse that had

two white foots and two brown foots mom and

dad was happy i didnt choose a loud bird!

~~~~~~~~~~~~~~~~~~~~~~~~~~~~~~~~~~~~~~~

                                          began
the baby chicks ~~beginned~~ to hatch very slowly.

      saw   poking
We ~~seen~~ their tiny beaks ~~pokeing~~ through the

                             heard   their
cracked shells, and we ~~heared~~ ~~they~~ tiny peeping.

      held
we ~~holded~~ our breaths and watched closely. all

       s were   knew
six egg ~~was~~ almost hatched. we ~~knowed~~ itd be so

                          babies
wonderful to see those ~~babys~~ being born!

Unit 9 • Paragraph 35
Errors

Apostrophes 1
Capitalization 4
Periods 1
Plurals 2
Pronouns 1
Verbs 7

Total Errors: 16

~~~~~~~~~~~~~~~~~~~~~~~~~~~~~~~~~~~~~~~

Mom and Dad said i could finally have a pet

                    took
of my own. They ~~taked~~ me to petes Pet Shop to

                              fish
pick one out. I looked at two ~~fishes~~ three birds

           mice   chose
and four ~~mouses~~. I ~~choosed~~ a mouse that had

            feet   feet
two white ~~foots~~ and two brown ~~foots~~ mom and

      were
dad ~~was~~ happy i didnt choose a loud bird!

Unit 9 • Paragraph 36
Errors

Apostrophes 2
Capitalization 5
Commas 2
Periods 2
Plurals 4
Verbs 3

Total Errors: 18

Ken and Alex pretended they was explorers on

a dangerous journey through the park city Zoo.

They hissed at snakes maked faces at the tigers,

and poked their fingers into many animals cages.

Thats when alexs mother comed up behind them

and said Whos ready for lunch.

"I could eat a horse shouted Henry. he hadnt

eaten much at Lunch. They serve fish sticks today,

and i wont' eat fish sticks he explained. Henry

looked through the pantry and the fridge. He

finded some cheese and crackers. "These will

make a nice snack he said

Ken and Alex pretended they ~~was~~ *were* explorers on

a dangerous journey through the ~~park city~~ Zoo.

They hissed at snakes, ~~maked~~ *made* faces at the tigers,

and poked their fingers into many animals' cages.

Thats when alexs mother ~~comed~~ *came* up behind them

and said "Whos ready for lunch?"

**Unit 10 • Paragraph 37
Errors**

Apostrophes. 4
Capitalization 3
Commas. 2
Question
  Marks. 1
Quotation
  Marks. 2
Verbs 3

Total Errors: 15

"I could eat a horse!" shouted Henry. he hadnt

eaten much at Lunch. "They served fish sticks today,

and i wont eat fish sticks" he explained. Henry

looked through the pantry and the fridge. He

~~finded~~ *found* some cheese and crackers. "These will

make a nice snack" he said.

**Unit 10 • Paragraph 38
Errors**

Apostrophes. 2
Capitalization 3
Commas. 2
Exclamation
  Points. 1
Periods. 1
Quotation
  Marks. 4
Verbs 2

Total Errors: 15

halloween is one of my favorrite holiday. Who wouldnt like scary costumes and candy. I cant wait to go from door to door around the neighborhood tonite. i'll probably ask, Trick or treat? about one hundred time

Wer'e going to the football game this Sunday. Stans dad is driving stan is bringing the sodas and Im making the sandwichs. We'll be rooting for the miami Dolphins to beat the Dallas cowboys. Me told Stan, lets get there early so we don't miss anything

halloween is one of my ~~favorrite~~ _favorite_ holiday**s**. Who

wouldnt' like scary costumes and candy**?** I cant**'** wait

to go from door to door around the neighborhood

~~tonite~~ _tonight_. **i'll** probably ask, "Trick or treat?" about one

hundred time**s**.

Unit 10 • Paragraph 39 Errors

Apostrophes..... 2
Capitalization 2
Periods......... 1
Plurals 2
Question
  Marks......... 1
Quotation
  Marks......... 2
Spelling 2

Total Errors: 12

We'r'e going to the football game this Sunday.

Stan's dad is driving**.** **stan** is bringing the sodas**,** and

Im' making the sandwich**e**s. We'll be rooting for the

miami Dolphins to beat the Dallas **cowboys**. ~~Me~~ **I**

told Stan, "**lets'** get there early so we don't miss

anything**.**"

Unit 10 • Paragraph 40 Errors

Apostrophes..... 4
Capitalization 4
Commas........ 2
Periods......... 1
Plurals 1
Pronouns 1
Quotation
  Marks......... 2

Total Errors: 15

The girl received a puppy for her birthday the furry puppy runned around in circles and then licked her face. this puppy is the best present ever cryed the little girl. "Hes so cute and cuddly" her said. im going to name him cuddles.

"I wish i had three wishes" allison said. With me first wish," she explained I would wish for a lot of toys. Then, i would wish for a big house to put all of my toy in" allison scratchd her head as her thinked hard about her final wish "I know she said, i would wish for three more wishs!"

The girl received a puppy for her birthday. the
                                            ran
furry puppy ~~runned~~ around in circles and then

licked her face. "this puppy is the best present
              "   cried
ever! ~~cryed~~ the little girl. "He's so cute and
         she   "
cuddly" ~~her~~ said. im going to name him cuddles."

Unit 11 • Paragraph 41
Errors

Apostrophes..... 2
Capitalization 4
Commas....... 1
Exclamation
   Points........ 1
Periods........ 1
Pronouns....... 1
Quotation
   Marks........ 4
Verbs 2

Total Errors: 16

"I wish i had three wishes" allison said. "With
my
~~me~~ first wish," she explained "I would wish for a

lot of toys. Then, i would wish for a big house to
                        s
put all of my toy in" allison scratchd her head as
she   thought
~~her~~ ~~thinked~~ hard about her final wish. "I know" she
         "   e
said, "i would wish for three more wishs!"

Unit 11 • Paragraph 42
Errors

Capitalization 5
Commas........ 3
Periods........ 2
Plurals 2
Pronouns....... 2
Quotation
   Marks........ 4
Verbs 2

Total Errors: 20

Sara pointed and whispered look over there

Her and Paul had just turned a corner on the

mountain trail. Lying in the grass next to the

trail was a small baby deer. it look at them

with wide eyes but didnt moove

April 1 2012, beginned as a calm day in mrs.

Lees class at oak grove Elementary School. Then

Joey suddenly jumped up pointed at Mrs lee, and

said, theres a huge spider crawling on you head"

The class gasped. Joey laugh and yelled, april

Fools!

Sara pointed and whispered "look over there.

She
~~Her~~ and Paul had just turned a corner on the

mountain trail. Lying in the grass next to the

trail was a small baby deer. it looked ~~look~~ at them

move
with wide eyes but didn't ~~moove~~.

Unit 11 • Paragraph 43
Errors

Apostrophes..... 1
Capitalization 2
Commas........ 1
Periods......... 2
Pronouns 1
Quotation
  Marks......... 2
Spelling 1
Verbs 1

Total Errors: 11

began
April 1, 2012, ~~beginned~~ as a calm day in mrs.

Lees class at oak grove Elementary School. Then

Joey suddenly jumped up, pointed at Mrs. lee, and

your
said, "there's a huge spider crawling on ~~you~~ head"!

laughed
The class gasped. Joey ~~laugh~~ and yelled, "april

Fools!"

Unit 11 • Paragraph 44
Errors

Apostrophes..... 2
Capitalization 6
Commas........ 2
Exclamation
  Points......... 1
Periods......... 1
Pronouns 1
Quotation
  Marks......... 3
Verbs 2

Total Errors: 18

Louisa may alcott writed a book titled Little women. The four sisters in the book is named Meg Jo Beth and amy They lives in an New england town during the time of the u s Civil War. Alcott based this book on her family.

Hans Christian Andersen was borned on april 2 1805 he was a author who is best known for his fairy tales. The titles of three of his most famous tale is "The ugly Duckling" "the Emperor's new Clothes," and The Snow queen

Louisa may alcott ~~writed~~ *wrote* a book titled <u>Little women</u>. The four sisters in the book ~~is~~ *are* named Meg, Jo, Beth, and amy. They lives in ~~an~~ *a* New england town during the time of the u. s. Civil War. Alcott based this book on her family.

Unit 12 • Paragraph 45
Errors

Capitalization 7
Commas 3
Periods 3
Underlines 1
Usage 1
Verbs 3

Total Errors: 18

Hans Christian Andersen was ~~borned~~ *born* on april 2, 1805. he was ~~a~~ *an* author who is best known for his fairy tales. The titles of three of his most famous tales *are* "The ugly Duckling," "the Emperor's new Clothes," and "The Snow queen."

Unit 12 • Paragraph 46
Errors

Capitalization 6
Commas 2
Periods 2
Plurals 1
Quotation
  Marks 2
Usage 1
Verbs 2

Total Errors: 16

Grandma smith taked her grandson to alaska when he was 11. They has a great adventure while they is there, and she wrote a book about it the book is called arctic son. Grandma Smith had the help of an artist who drawed wonderful pictures of whales wolfs and many walrus.

Tammy Troy and me sit around last night watching movies we began the evening with Star wars. Then we watched finding nemo. We was going to watch eragon next, but we all fall asleep

Grandma smith ~~taked~~ (took) her grandson to alaska

when he was 11. They ~~has~~ (had) a great adventure

while they ~~was~~ (were) there, and she wrote a book about

it. the book is called arctic son. Grandma Smith

had the help of an artist who ~~drawed~~ (drew) wonderful

pictures of whales, ~~wolfs~~ (wolves) and many ~~walrus.~~ (walruses)

Unit 12 • Paragraph 47
Errors

Capitalization 5
Commas. 2
Periods. 1
Plurals 2
Underlines 1
Verbs 4

Total Errors: 15

Tammy, Troy, and ~~me sit~~ (I sat) around last night

watching movies, we began the evening with

Star wars. Then we watched finding nemo.

We ~~was~~ (were) going to watch eragon next, but

we all ~~fail~~ (fell) asleep.

Unit 12 • Paragraph 48
Errors

Capitalization 5
Commas. 2
Periods. 2
Pronouns 1
Underlines 3
Verbs 3

Total Errors: 16

Fishing is fun for many reasons? It is relax to bee in a boat out on a lake or in a stream inn the woods these is places that usually offer piece and quiet. Catching fish is another grate thing about fishing. Nothing tastes better than fresh fish cooked over a open fire.

My best friend is named ella. I seen her every day last summer when we was at camp i hope she rights to me over the school year. I cant weight until next Summer when her and me will be at Blue river Camp together.

Fishing is fun for many reasons? It is ~~relax~~ *relaxing* to

bee in a boat out on a lake or in a stream in

the woods these ~~is~~ *are* places that usually offer ~~piece~~ *peace*

and quiet. Catching fish is another ~~grate~~ *great* thing

about fishing. Nothing tastes better than fresh

fish cooked over ~~a~~ *an* open fire.

Unit 13 • Paragraph 49
Errors

Capitalization 1
Homophones 4
Periods......... 2
Usage......... 2
Verbs 1

Total Errors: 10

My best friend is named ella. I ~~seen~~ *saw* her every

day last summer when we ~~was~~ *were* at camp i hope

she ~~rights~~ *writes* to me over the school year. I cant

~~weight~~ *wait* until next Summer when ~~her~~ *she* and ~~me~~ *I* will

be at Blue river Camp together.

Unit 13 • Paragraph 50
Errors

Apostrophes..... 1
Capitalization 4
Homophones 2
Periods......... 1
Pronouns 2
Verbs 2

Total Errors: 12

Snow was falling outside. Lane and sam wanted

to go play, but them didnt have sleds. Their father

sayed, I ll find you each a sled." He come back

with too lids from they're trashcans. "last won to

the hill is a frozen snowman! their father shouting.

I stubbed my tow while stumbling out of

bed this morning. Ouch? i yelled. Then my cat

scratched me when I go to pet her the scratch

actually drew blood, so I went to the bathroom

to get a bandage. Thats when I triped over my

brothers skateboard it was shapeing up to be

a ruff day.

Snow was falling outside. Lane and sam wanted

to go play, but ~~them~~ *they* **didnt have sleds. Their father**

~~sayed~~ *said*, **"I'll find you each a sled." He** ~~come~~ *came* **back**

with ~~too~~ *two* **lids from** ~~they're~~ *their* **trashcans. "last** ~~won~~ *one* **to**

the hill is a frozen snowman! their father ~~shouting~~ *shouted***.**

Unit 13 • Paragraph 51 Errors

Apostrophes	2
Capitalization	2
Homophones	3
Pronouns	1
Quotation Marks	2
Verbs	3

Total Errors: 13

I stubbed my ~~tow~~ *toe* **while stumbling out of**

bed this morning. "Ouch?" i yelled. Then my cat

scratched me when I ~~go~~ *went* **to pet her the scratch**

actually drew blood, so I went to the bathroom

to get a bandage. Thats when I triped over my

brothers skateboard it was ~~shapeing~~ *shaping* **up to be**

a ~~ruff~~ *rough* **day.**

Unit 13 • Paragraph 52 Errors

Apostrophes	2
Capitalization	3
Exclamation Points	1
Homophones	2
Periods	2
Quotation Marks	2
Verbs	3

Total Errors: 15

Lets build a clubhouse in the back yard, said Tina. Jack asked what can we use to make are house. Just then, Tinas mother bringed two giant cardboard box outside to throw away. Tina and jack new exactly what to do with those boxs.

Unit 14
Paragraph
53

Alex and kay was running threw the house. "Dont run into the kitchen, their older sister said but they kept runing until they both slipped and fell on the kitchen floor. Their sister standed over them with a mop and a bucket of water. Maybe you two shouldve listened" she say with a smile.

Unit 14
Paragraph
54

"Lets build a clubhouse in the back yard," said

Tina. Jack asked "what can we use to make ~~are~~ *our*

house." Just then, Tinas mother ~~bringed~~ *brought* two giant

cardboard ~~box~~ *boxes* outside to throw away. Tina and

jack ~~new~~ *knew* exactly what to do with those boxs.

Unit 14 • Paragraph 53 Errors

Apostrophes 2
Capitalization 2
Commas 1
Homophones 2
Plurals 2
Question
  Marks 1
Quotation
  Marks 4
Verbs 1

Total Errors: 15

Alex and kay ~~was~~ *were* running ~~threw~~ *through* the house.

"Dont run into the kitchen," their older sister said

but they kept ~~runing~~ *running* until they both slipped and

fell on the kitchen floor. Their sister ~~standed~~ *stood* over

them with a mop and a bucket of water. "Maybe

you two shouldve listened" she ~~say~~ *said* with a smile.

Unit 14 • Paragraph 54 Errors

Apostrophes 2
Capitalization 1
Commas 2
Homophones 1
Quotation
  Marks 2
Verbs 4

Total Errors: 12

a fish was swimming in the see. The fish seen

a hook with a worm on it and was about to take

a bite "Please dont eat me cryed the wiggling

worm. The fish felt bad for the worm and he

swimmed away. Two little creatures was saved

that day

John and his family flied on an airplane to

chicago illinois. John sat near a window during the

flight. He shouted I can sea the Atlantic ocean!"

as the plain flew over water. His sister shaked

her head and replies, "I think thats actually

Lake michigan."

a fish was swimming in the ~~see~~ [sea]. The fish ~~seen~~ [saw]

a hook with a worm on it and was about to take

a bite⊙ "Please don~~t~~ ['] eat me!" ~~cryed~~ [cried] the wiggling

worm. The fish felt bad for the worm⊙ [,] and he

~~swimmed~~ [swam] away. Two little creatures ~~was~~ [were] saved

that day⊙

Unit 14 • Paragraph 55 Errors

Apostrophes	1
Capitalization	1
Commas	1
Exclamation Points	1
Homophones	1
Periods	2
Quotation Marks	1
Verbs	4

Total Errors: 12

John and his family ~~flied~~ [flew] on an airplane to

chicago⊙ [,] illinois. John sat near a window during the

flight. He shouted⊙ [,] "I can ~~sea~~ [see] the Atlantic ocean!"

as the ~~plain~~ [plane] flew over water. His sister ~~shaked~~ [shook]

her head and ~~replies~~ [replied], "I think that~~s~~ ['] actually

Lake michigan."

Unit 14 • Paragraph 56 Errors

Apostrophes	1
Capitalization	4
Commas	2
Homophones	2
Quotation Marks	1
Verbs	3

Total Errors: 13

Kevin and Bob wanted to play pirates. They had a small chest but they didnt have no treasure. Kevin had a idea. Him filled the chest with pennys from the penny jar. "Now were pirates said kevin and bob.

Boyd and jessica ride they skateboards to school each day. Both childs always ware helmets kneepads and elbow pads They promised their mother that they wouldn't never cross a street without look both ways. She's proud of how safe they is

Kevin and Bob wanted to play pirates. They

had a small chest, but they didn't have ~~no~~ *any* treasure.

Kevin had ~~a~~ *an* idea. ~~Him~~ *He* filled the chest with ~~pennys~~ *pennies*

from the penny jar. "Now we're pirates," said ~~kevin~~ Kevin

and ~~bob~~ Bob.

Unit 15 • Paragraph 57 Errors

Apostrophes 2
Capitalization 2
Commas 2
Double
  Negatives 1
Plurals 1
Pronouns 1
Quotation
  Marks 1
Usage 1

Total Errors: 11

Boyd and ~~jessica~~ Jessica ride ~~they~~ *their* skateboards to

school each day. Both ~~childs~~ *children* always ~~ware~~ *wear* helmets,

kneepads, and elbow pads. They promised their

mother that they wouldn't ~~never~~ ever cross a street

without ~~look~~ *looking* both ways. She's proud of how safe

they ~~is~~ *are*.

Unit 15 • Paragraph 58 Errors

Capitalization 1
Commas 2
Double
  Negatives 1
Homophones 1
Periods 2
Plurals 1
Pronouns 1
Verbs 2

Total Errors: 11

My class went to Mr franks farm on tuesday february 3. We see cows chickens and horses. I won't never forget when Mr. Frank asked if any of us wood like to ride a horse. I screamed, "I would." I got to be the first one to ride what a thrill.

J.D. and me went to see a movie called Robby the robot. The problem was that j d forgetted his wallet. He didn't have no money. I said, I dont has enough for both of us." Us didn't get to see no movie that day.

My class went to Mr. franks farm on tuesday february 3. We ~~see~~ *saw* **cows chickens and horses. I won't** ~~never~~ **forget when Mr. Frank asked if any of us** ~~wood~~ *would* **like to ride a horse. I screamed, "I would." I got to be the first one to ride what a thrill.**

Unit 15 • Paragraph 59 Errors

Apostrophes	1
Capitalization	4
Commas	3
Double Negatives	1
Exclamation Points	2
Homophones	1
Periods	2
Verbs	1

Total Errors: 15

J.D. and ~~me~~ *I* **went to see a movie called Robby the robot. The problem was that** ~~j d~~ ~~forgetted~~ *forgot* **his wallet. He didn't have** ~~no~~ *any* **money. I said, "I dont have enough for both of us." ** ~~Us~~ *We* **didn't get to see** ~~no~~ *a* **movie that day.**

Unit 15 • Paragraph 60 Errors

Apostrophes	1
Capitalization	3
Double Negatives	2
Periods	2
Pronouns	2
Quotation Marks	1
Underlines	1
Verbs	2

Total Errors: 14

Do you has any warm sweater that are made of wool. If so, you mite want to thank a sheep. Wool from sheeps coats has been knit woven and sewn into products for many centurys wool is soft and warm. It resists fire and can be easily storred

Historys most famous mummy, is King Tut. He is a teenager when he died this was over 4,000 year ago. Him was in a secret tomb that scientists did not fined until 1922. King tuts mummy lay inside a sollid gold coffin

Do you ~~has~~ (have) any warm sweater(s) that are made

of wool(?) If so, you ~~mite~~ (might) want to thank a sheep.

Wool from sheep's coats has been knit(,) woven(,)

and sewn into products for many ~~centurys~~ (centuries) wool

is soft and warm. It resists fire and can be

easily ~~storred~~ (stored)(.)

Unit 16 • Paragraph 61 Errors

Apostrophes..... 1
Capitalization 1
Commas........ 2
Homophones 1
Periods......... 2
Plurals 2
Question
  Marks......... 1
Spelling 1
Verbs 1

Total Errors: 12

History's most famous mummy(,) is King Tut. He

~~is~~ (was) a teenager when he died(.) this was over 4,000

year(s) ago. ~~Him~~ (He) was in a secret tomb that scientists

did not ~~fined~~ (find) until 1922. King tut's mummy lay

inside a ~~sollid~~ (solid) gold coffin(.)

Unit 16 • Paragraph 62 Errors

Apostrophes..... 2
Capitalization 2
Commas........ 1
Homophones 1
Periods......... 2
Plurals 1
Pronouns 1
Spelling 1
Verbs 1

Total Errors: 12

The first presidential election in america taked place on January 7 1789. The person who winned that election was a general in the army he helpped the United states gain independence from Great Britain. Do you no who was elected on that date in history.

On July 20 1969 Neil armstrong climed down a ladder. Millions of person watch him on their television sets. As he stepped off the ladder, him said Thats one small step for man, one jiant leap for mankind." Neil was the first human to set foot on are moon.

The first presidential election in america ~~taked~~ *took*

place on January 7, 1789. The person who ~~winned~~ *won*

that election was a general in the army, he ~~helpped~~ *helped*

the United states gain independence from Great

Britain. Do you ~~no~~ *know* who was elected on that date

in history?

Unit 16 • Paragraph 63
Errors

Capitalization 3
Commas 1
Homophones 1
Periods 1
Question
 Marks 1
Verbs 3

Total Errors: 10

On July 20, 1969, Neil armstrong ~~climed~~ *climbed* down

a ladder. Millions of ~~person~~ *people* watch*ed* him on their

television sets. As he stepped off the ladder, ~~him~~ *he*

said, "That's one small step for man, one ~~jiant~~ *giant* leap

for mankind." Neil was the first human to set foot

on ~~are~~ *our* moon.

Unit 16 • Paragraph 64
Errors

Apostrophes 1
Capitalization 1
Commas 3
Homophones 1
Pronouns 1
Plurals 1
Quotation
 Marks 1
Spelling 2
Verbs 1

Total Errors: 12

Mom maked a pitcher of lemonade and put it

on the kichen table. She turn to wipe her hand's

on a towel when she herd a lowd crash. Our crazy

cat had jumped onto the table and nocked over

the pitcher mom shaked her head and began

to clean up the spill.

"It's snowing screamed Ralph. "Lets make a

snow family." He grabed carrots for the noses and

some raisin for the eyes. Him and his sister then

ran outside and began rolling giant balls of Snow.

Soon them had made a mom a dad a sun and a

daughter.

Mom ~~maked~~ (made) **a pitcher of lemonade and put it on the** ~~kichen~~ (kitchen) **table. She** turn (ed) **to wipe her** ~~hand's~~ (hands) **on a towel when she** ~~herd~~ (heard) **a** ~~lowd~~ (loud) **crash. Our crazy cat had jumped onto the table and** (k)nocked **over the pitcher**⊙ **mom** (shook) ~~shaked~~ **her head and began to clean up the spill.**

Unit 17 • Paragraph 65 Errors	
Apostrophes	1
Capitalization	1
Homophones	1
Periods	1
Spelling	3
Verbs	3

Total Errors: 10

"It's snowing!**" screamed Ralph. "Let**'**s make a snow family." He** ~~grabed~~ (grabbed) **carrots for the noses and some** raisin(s) **for the eyes.** ~~Him~~ (He) **and his sister then ran outside and began rolling giant balls of** /snow. **Soon** ~~them~~ (they) **had made a mom**, **a dad**, **a** ~~sun~~ (son), **and a daughter.**

Unit 17 • Paragraph 66 Errors	
Apostrophes	1
Capitalization	1
Commas	3
Exclamation Points	1
Homophones	1
Pronouns	2
Plurals	1
Quotation Marks	1
Verbs	1

Total Errors: 12

the Vancouver Aquarium in canada is a great place to sea white whales. These beautiful creature have stout bodys and small head and they breathe threw a blowhole. Though these whales spend most of there time in the cold arctic ocean, they swim down to warmer waters during the Summer.

Shelly writed a poem called An Early Spring. She telled Tina and I that its about her favorite time of year. She said that Spring is when the sun is shining the flours are blooming and everyones smileing.

the Vancouver Aquarium in canada is a

great place to ~~sea~~ *see* white whales. These beautiful

creature*s* have stout ~~bodys~~ *bodies* and small head*s* and

they breathe ~~threw~~ *through* a blowhole. Though these

whales spend most of ~~there~~ *their* time in the cold arctic

ocean, they swim down to warmer waters during

the Summer.

Unit 17 • Paragraph 67
Errors

Capitalization 5
Commas........ 1
Homophones 3
Plurals 3

Total Errors: 12

Shelly ~~writed~~ *wrote* a poem called "An Early Spring."

She ~~telled~~ *told* Tina and ~~I~~ *me* that its about her favorite

time of year. She said that Spring is when

the sun is shining, the ~~flours~~ *flowers* are blooming, and

everyone*s* ~~smileing~~ *smiling*.

Unit 17 • Paragraph 68
Errors

Apostrophes..... 2
Capitalization 1
Commas........ 2
Homophones 1
Pronouns 1
Quotation
   Marks......... 2
Verbs 3

Total Errors: 12

My name is Jason and I live on Waterlily lane. I have two best friend and I like to play baseball with them until me mom calls me in for dinner. After my family eat's, my job is to clear the dishs from the table. Than i do my homework, witch I usually finish by nine oclock.

Officer Roberts has been a policeman for over ate years. He won a medal last weak for chaseing two thiefs who stealed the mayor's wifes purse. Officer roberts said It's a honor to recieve this medal.

My name is Jason, and I live on Waterlily lane.

I have two best friend and I like to play baseball

with them until ~~me~~ my mom calls me in for dinner.

After my family ~~eat's~~ eats, my job is to clear the dishs

from the table. ~~Than~~ Then ~~i~~ I do my homework, ~~witch~~ which I

usually finish by nine o'clock.

Unit 18 • Paragraph 69 Errors

Apostrophes	2
Capitalization	2
Commas	2
Homophones	2
Plurals	2
Pronouns	1

Total Errors: 11

Officer Roberts has been a policeman for over

~~ate~~ eight years. He won a medal last ~~weak~~ week for ~~chaseing~~ chasing

two ~~thiefs~~ thieves who ~~stealed~~ stole the mayor's wifes purse.

Officer ~~roberts~~ Roberts said "It's ~~a~~ an honor to ~~recieve~~ receive this

medal."

Unit 18 • Paragraph 70 Errors

Apostrophes	1
Capitalization	1
Commas	1
Homophones	2
Plurals	1
Quotation Marks	2
Spelling	1
Usage	1
Verbs	2

Total Errors: 12

My younger brother jackie can be a big pane.

He snoops around in my room and gos through

my desk drawers. He leaves my clothes papers

and books in a mess. He doesnt know when to

be serious. He always sprays me with the hoes

whenever were washing mr Hill's car

Theres a boy in my grade who is the goodest

football player in our town. He is a fantastic

athlete but he isnt always a good teammate. When

his teem looses a game, he crys and blame

everyone else our coachs have to talk to him

after every loss.

My younger brother jackie can be a big ~~pane~~. *pain*

He snoops around in my room and ~~gos~~ through *goes*

my desk drawers. He leaves my clothes, papers,

and books in a mess. He doesn't know when to

be serious. He always sprays me with the ~~hoes~~ *hose*

whenever we're washing mr. Hill's car.

Unit 18 • Paragraph 71
Errors

Apostrophes 2
Capitalization 2
Commas 2
Homophones 2
Periods 2
Verbs 1

Total Errors: 11

There's a boy in my grade who is the ~~goodest~~ *best*

football player in our town. He is a fantastic

athlete, but he isn't always a good teammate. When

his ~~teem~~ ~~looses~~ a game, he ~~crys~~ and blames *team* *loses* *cries*

everyone else. our coaches have to talk to him

after every loss.

Unit 18 • Paragraph 72
Errors

Apostrophes 2
Capitalization 1
Commas 1
Homophones 1
Periods 1
Plurals 1
Spelling 1
Usage 1
Verbs 2

Total Errors: 11

did you know that herding dog come in many

shape and sizes. They can be tall or short the

shortest herding dogs were bred to heard cattle.

Their short legs move quickly when they running

around the herd, and they smaller bodys can avoid

a kick from a angry cow.

My family and me went over to Mrs Fox house

the other day. She baked the greatest desert

Ive ever eated. It was a pie that was filled with

blueberrys, raspberrys, peachs, and several other

type of fruit. She served it warm with a enormous

scoop of Vanilla ice cream.

did you know that herding dog^s come in many

shape^s and sizes? They can be tall or short. the

shortest herding dogs were bred to ~~heard~~ *herd* cattle.

Their short legs move quickly when they ~~running~~ *run*

around the herd, and ~~they~~ *their* smaller ~~bodys~~ *bodies* can avoid

a kick from ~~a~~ *an* angry cow.

Unit 19 • Paragraph 73 Errors

Capitalization	2
Homophones	1
Periods	1
Plurals	3
Pronouns	1
Question Marks	1
Usage	1
Verbs	1

Total Errors: 11

My family and ~~me~~ *I* went over to Mrs. Fox^'s house

the other day. She baked the greatest ~~desert~~ *dessert*

I've ever ~~eated~~ *eaten*. It was a pie that was filled with

~~blueberrys~~ *blueberries*, ~~raspberrys~~ *raspberries*, peach^es, and several other

type^s of fruit. She served it warm with ~~a~~ *an* enormous

scoop of Vanilla ice cream.

Unit 19 • Paragraph 74 Errors

Apostrophes	2
Capitalization	1
Homophones	1
Periods	1
Plurals	4
Pronouns	1
Usage	1
Verbs	1

Total Errors: 12

Name: _____ Date: _____

Gooses fly south for the Winter. They fly together, and the group forms the shape of the letter V. As each bird flaps it's wings, the wind it make lifts the bird that follows behined. They work as a team and this helps them travel faster. The goose inn the front of the groop drops back when it get tired

Forests can be finded all over the world, and many different animals spend they're lifes in them. Small animal that live in the forrest eat the fruits nuts mushrooms and insects found there. The larger animals of the forest eats the smaller animals?

~~~~~~

Geese
~~Gooses~~ fly south for the W/inter. They fly together, and the group forms the shape of the letter V. As each bird flaps ~~it's~~ *its* wings, the wind it make *s* lifts the bird that follows ~~behined.~~ *behind* They work as a team *,* and this helps them travel faster. The goose ~~inn~~ *in* the front of the ~~groop~~ *group* drops back when it get *s* tired *.*

Unit 19 • Paragraph 75 Errors	
Capitalization	1
Commas	1
Homophones	2
Periods	1
Plurals	1
Spelling	2
Verbs	2

Total Errors: 10

~~~~~~

Forests can be ~~finded~~ *found* all over the world, and many different animals spend ~~they're~~ *their* ~~lifes~~ *lives* in them. Small animal *s* that live in the ~~forrest~~ *forest* eat the fruits *,* nuts *,* mushrooms *,* and insects found there. The larger animals of the forest eat*s*/ the smaller animals *.* ?

Unit 19 • Paragraph 76 Errors	
Commas	3
Homophones	1
Periods	1
Plurals	2
Spelling	1
Verbs	2

Total Errors: 10

Brian is teaching heself how to play guitar. He begin each lesson by watching a video that shows the correct fingger positions. Than he picks up his guitar and starts struming it sounds awful. He shood probably take lessens from a pro.

Unit 20
Paragraph
77

Steve and me learned to do many new thing at camp this summer. We was taught how to canoe build a fire and make a shelter. We also meet three funny freinds named Billy Bobby and benny. This was their first time at camp, to. We all had a great Summer.

Unit 20
Paragraph
78

Brian is teaching ~~heself~~ [himself] how to play guitar. He

begin[s] each lesson by watching a video that shows

the correct ~~fingger~~ [finger] positions. ~~Than~~ [Then] he picks up his

guitar and starts ~~struming~~ [strumming]. it sounds awful. He

~~shood~~ [should] probably take ~~lessens~~ [lessons] from a pro.

Unit 20 • Paragraph 77
Errors

Capitalization 1
Exclamation
  Points. 1
Homophones 2
Periods. 1
Pronouns 1
Spelling 2
Verbs 2

Total Errors: 10

Steve and ~~me~~ [I] learned to do many new thing[s]

at camp this summer. We ~~was~~ [were] taught how to

canoe, build a fire, and make a shelter. We also

~~meet~~ [met] three funny ~~freinds~~ [friends] named Billy, Bobby, and

benny. This was their first time at camp, ~~to~~. [too] We

all had a great [S]ummer.

Unit 20 • Paragraph 78
Errors

Capitalization 2
Commas. 4
Homophones 1
Plurals 1
Pronouns 1
Spelling 1
Verbs 2

Total Errors: 12

How exciting. A famous photographer named Miles Shutterbug is comeing to our school. Hes known for takeing amazing pictures of frogs lizzards, and butterfly. He will be driving thru our town on the Friday before Valentines day.

Wood you like to know how to make a tasty taco salad you should first tare some lettuce into a bowl. Then you should cut up some tomato green pepper and olives. Add greated cheese cooked hamburger, and broken tortilla chips. Toss it toogether and add a special mexican salad dressing.

How exciting! A famous photographer named

Miles Shutterbug is ~~comeing~~ *coming* to our school. He's

known for ~~takeing~~ *taking* amazing pictures of frogs,

~~lizzards~~ *lizards*, and ~~butterfly~~ *butterflies*. He will be driving ~~thru~~ *through*

our town on the Friday before Valentine's day.

Unit 20 • Paragraph 79
Errors

Apostrophes. 2
Capitalization 1
Commas. 1
Exclamation
 Points. 1
Plurals 1
Spelling 2
Verbs 2

Total Errors: 10

~~Wood~~ *Would* you like to know how to make a tasty

taco salad? you should first ~~tare~~ *tear* some lettuce into

a bowl. Then you should cut up some tomato,

green pepper, and olives. Add ~~greated~~ *grated* cheese,

cooked hamburger, and broken tortilla chips.

Toss it ~~toogether~~ *together* and add a special mexican

salad dressing.

Unit 20 • Paragraph 80
Errors

Capitalization 2
Commas. 3
Homophones 2
Question
 Marks. 1
Spelling 2

Total Errors: 10

Its important to know the rules of baseball before u start playing. Fore example, you should know witch direction to run after you hit the ball. Don't you agree that is a importent thing to know. My friend run strait to third base one time. Him and I still laugh about it.

The railroad pass through a tiny town named sunnyville the town only has a gas station a barbershop and a small store called barney's market. Barneys is small, but them make the best homemade ice cream youll ever eat. Go there if your ever in town and in the mood for a creamy treat.

Its important to know the rules of baseball

before ~~u~~ *you* start playing. Fore *(e)* example, you should

know ~~witch~~ *which* direction to run after you hit the ball.

Don't you agree that is ~~a importent~~ *an important* thing to know *(?)*

My friend ~~run strait~~ *ran straight* to third base one time. ~~Him~~ *He*

and I still laugh about it.

**Unit 21 • Paragraph 81
Errors**

Apostrophes 1
Homophones 3
Pronouns 1
Question
  Marks 1
Spelling 2
Usage 1
Verbs 1

Total Errors: 10

The railroad ~~pass~~ *passes* through a tiny town named

sunnyville the town only has a gas station(,) a

barbershop(,) and a small store called barney's

market. Barney's is small, but ~~them~~ *they* make the

best homemade ice cream youll ever eat. Go

there if ~~your~~ *you're* ever in town and in the mood

for a creamy treat.

**Unit 21 • Paragraph 82
Errors**

Apostrophes 2
Capitalization 4
Commas 2
Homophones 1
Periods 1
Pronouns 1
Verbs 1

Total Errors: 12

On Febuary 20 1962 a astronaut named john Glenn became the first american to orbit Earth.

That was just one of Glenns many accomplishment.

He later was elected to the U S Senate and in 1998 he becomed the oldest man to fly in space.

He was 77 year old at the time.

On July 15, 2012 my family and me go to visit are relatives in Cincinnati ohio. Their house is at 3540 Sycamore st. Aunt Sue and uncle Bart live there with there five childs. The kids names is Pat Lana Joe Darla, and Opal.

On Febuary 20, 1962, ~~a~~ *an* astronaut named john

Glenn became the first american to orbit Earth.

That was just one of Glenn's many accomplishment*s*.

He later was elected to the U. S. Senate, and in

1998 he ~~becomed~~ *became* the oldest man to fly in space.

He was 77 year*s* old at the time.

Unit 21 • Paragraph 83
Errors

Apostrophes 1
Capitalization 2
Commas 3
Periods 2
Plurals 2
Spelling 1
Usage 1
Verbs 1

Total Errors: 13

On July 15, 2012, my family and ~~me go~~ *I went* to visit

~~are~~ *our* relatives in Cincinnati, ohio. Their house is at

3540 Sycamore st. Aunt Sue and uncle Bart live

there with ~~there~~ *their* five ~~childs~~ *children*. The kids' names ~~is~~ *are*

Pat, Lana, Joe, Darla, and Opal.

Unit 21 • Paragraph 84
Errors

Apostrophes 1
Capitalization 3
Commas 5
Homophones 2
Plurals 1
Pronouns 1
Verbs 2

Total Errors: 15

It was a clear knight, and Sadie was looking
up at the sky. She gasped as a falling star shooted
across the black night. Should i make a wish?
Sadie asked? Sadies sister sayed "Only if you
promise to tell me what u wished for"

Dad and Tom spended all of yesterday mowing
the lawn, rakeing the leafs, and trimming the trees.
It take allmost four ours. They rewarded themselfs
with a extra large pizza topped with sausage
pepperoni and bacon. Toms dad said Now let's
relax and watch Tv.

It was a clear ~~knight~~, and Sadie was looking up at the sky. She gasped as a falling star ~~shooted~~ *shot* across the black night. "Should **i** make a wish?" Sadie asked~~?~~ **Sadie's** sister ~~sayed~~ *said* "Only if you promise to tell me what ~~u~~ *you* wished for"

Unit 22 • Paragraph 85 Errors

Apostrophes..... 1
Capitalization 1
Commas......... 1
Homophones 1
Periods......... 2
Quotation
  Marks......... 2
Spelling 1
Verbs 2

Total Errors: 11

Dad and Tom ~~spended~~ *spent* all of yesterday mowing the lawn, ~~rakeing~~ *raking* the ~~leafs~~ *leaves*, and trimming the trees. It ~~take~~ *took* ~~allmost~~ *almost* four ~~ours~~ *hours*. They rewarded ~~themselfs~~ *themselves* with ~~a~~ *an* extra large pizza topped with sausage pepperoni and bacon. **Tom's** dad said "Now let's relax and watch **Tv**."

Unit 22 • Paragraph 86 Errors

Apostrophes..... 1
Capitalization 1
Commas......... 3
Homophones 1
Plurals 1
Pronouns 1
Quotation
  Marks......... 2
Spelling 1
Usage.......... 1
Verbs 3

Total Errors: 15

Kim, Kirk, and me went to the beech. We applyed sunscreen as soon as we got their. Then we had a day of fun in the sun. We builded sandcastles ran along the sand and splashed in the wayves. We was starving by 115 pm. Luckily, we had packed a picnick lunch.

Sally finded an old box hidden in one corner of the attic at her aunts house. She opened it and sees a string of pearls, two boxs of gold coins, and a album full of old picture sally grabed the album and raced downstairs to show her ant

Kim, Kirk, and ~~me~~ *I* went to the ~~beech~~ *beach*. We ~~applyed~~ *applied* sunscreen as soon as we got ~~their~~ *there*. Then we had a day of fun in the sun. We ~~builded~~ *built* sandcastles ⊙ ran along the sand ⊙ and splashed in the ~~wayves~~ *waves*. We ~~was~~ *were* starving by 1٨15 p٨m ⊙ Luckily, we had packed a picnick̸ lunch.

Unit 22 • Paragraph 87
Errors

Colons	1
Commas	2
Homophones	2
Periods	1
Pronouns	1
Spelling	2
Verbs	3

Total Errors: 12

Sally ~~finded~~ *found* an old box hidden in one corner of the attic at her aunt٨'s house. She opened it and ~~sees~~ *saw* a string of pearls, two box٨es of gold coins, and ~~a~~ *an* album full of old picture٨s ⊙ ṣ̲ally ~~grabed~~ *grabbed* the album and raced downstairs to show her ~~ant~~ *aunt* ⊙

Unit 22 • Paragraph 88
Errors

Apostrophes	1
Capitalization	1
Homophones	1
Periods	2
Plurals	2
Usage	1
Verbs	3

Total Errors: 11

I carefully readed the directions on the boxx

for how to make pancakes. I puts the mix, some

milk two egg, and sum oil in a bowl. I stired

those ingredients together. Than I poored small

circles of the batter onto a hot griddle and cooked

them until they was golden brown. It was so

delicious

Barn owls is fully grown by about twelve

weeks of age. They open they eyes after three

week grow feathers after six weaks, and practice

flying after ate weeks. Bye the twelth week,

their reddy to leave the nest and hunt for food

on there own

I carefully ~~readed~~ read the directions on the box~~x~~

for how to make pancakes. I put~~s~~ the mix, some

milk, two egg~~s~~, and ~~sum~~ some oil in a bowl. I sti~~r~~red

those ingredients together. ~~Than~~ Then I ~~poored~~ poured small

circles of the batter onto a hot griddle and cooked

them until they ~~was~~ were golden brown. It was so

delicious!

Unit 23 • Paragraph 89
Errors

Commas 1
Exclamation
  Points 1
Homophones 2
Plurals 1
Spelling 2
Verbs 4

Total Errors: 11

Barn owls ~~is~~ are fully grown by about twelve

weeks of age. They open ~~they~~ their eyes after three

week~~s~~ grow feathers after six ~~weaks~~ weeks, and practice

flying after ~~ate~~ eight weeks. By~~e~~ the twelfth week,

~~their reddy~~ they're ready to leave the nest and hunt for food

on ~~there~~ their own.

Unit 23 • Paragraph 90
Errors

Commas 1
Homophones 5
Periods 1
Plurals 1
Pronouns 1
Spelling 2
Verbs 1

Total Errors: 12

Becky babysitted the Cooper twins last knight.

She get payed $15 a hour to watch Nate and Nick

cooper every friday night so that they're parents

can see a movie. Both boys' love playing video

games and watching Sesame Street on TV. Becky

doesnt mined her job at all.

It rain all day yesterday. We were board and

we didn't have nothing to do. Thats when I come

up with the idea of playing bored games. We

played Chutes and ladders Monopoly, and cranium

it was fun, but I really hope it don't rein

tomorrow.

Becky ~~babysitted~~ **the Cooper twins last** ~~knight~~. *(babysat)* *(night)*

She get ~~payed~~ **$15** ~~a~~ **hour to watch Nate and Nick** *(gets)* *(paid)* *(an)*

cooper every friday night so that ~~they're~~ **parents** *(their)*

can see a movie. Both boys' love playing video

games and watching <u>Sesame Street</u> **on TV. Becky**

doesn't ~~mined~~ **her job at all.** *(mind)*

It rain **all day yesterday. We were** ~~board~~ **and** *(ed)* *(bored)*

we didn't have ~~nothing~~ **to do. That's when I** ~~come~~ *(anything)* *(came)*

up with the idea of playing ~~bored~~ **games. We** *(board)*

played Chutes and ladders, Monopoly, and cranium.

it was fun, but I really hope it ~~don't rein~~ *(doesn't rain)*

tomorrow.

Will wanted to make sandwichs for next weeks lunches, so he went to the store to bye a few things. He bot two different loafs of bread a pound of turkey and half a pound of swiss cheese. He compleated his shopping trip buy picking up sum lettuce and tomatos.

Did you know that a hare is a kind of rabbit i learned this when we red a story called The Tortoise And The Hare. Its about a race between a slow turtle and a speedy hair. Can you guess who won. Would you beleave that the slowwer animal win the race?

Will wanted to make sandwichs^e for next week's

lunches, so he went to the store to ~~bye~~ *buy* a few

things. He ~~bot~~ *bought* two different ~~leafs~~ *loaves* of bread, a pound

of turkey, and half a pound of swiss cheese. He

~~compleated~~ *completed* his shopping trip ~~buy~~ *by* picking up ~~sum~~ *some*

lettuce and tomatos^e.

Unit 24 • Paragraph 93 Errors

Apostrophes. 1
Capitalization 1
Commas. 2
Homophones 3
Plurals 3
Spelling 2

Total Errors: 12

Did you know that a hare is a kind of rabbit?

~~i~~ learned this when we ~~red~~ *read* a story called "The

Tortoise ~~And~~ The Hare." It's about a race between

a slow turtle and a speedy ~~hair~~ *hare*. Can you guess

who won? Would you ~~beleave~~ *believe* that the ~~slowwer~~ *slower*

animal ~~win~~ *wins* the race?

Unit 24 • Paragraph 94 Errors

Apostrophes. 1
Capitalization 3
Homophones 2
Question
  Marks. 2
Quotation
  Marks. 2
Spelling 2
Verbs 1

Total Errors: 13

During the 1930s, oklahoma and parts of Kansas, Texas, Colorado, and New mexico had terible dust storms. Many farmer was forced to pack up there families and leave they headed to California, wear they hoped to fined work.

My class was supposed to go on a feeled trip to prairie park yesterday. My teacher said The bus will be arriveing at 800 am." We weighted for a hour, but no bus never showed up. We later learned that the bus breaked down on it's way to our school. We was all vary disappointed.

During the 1930s, oklahoma and parts of

Kansas, Texas, Colorado, and New mexico had

terrible ~~teribie~~ dust storms. Many farmer**s** ~~was~~ **were** forced to

pack up ~~there~~ **their** families and leave⊙ they headed to

California, ~~wear~~ **where** they hoped to ~~fined~~ **find** work.

**Unit 24 • Paragraph 95
Errors**

Capitalization 3
Homophones 3
Periods. 1
Plurals 1
Spelling 1
Verbs 1

Total Errors: 10

My class was supposed to go on a ~~feeld~~ **field** trip

to prairie park yesterday. My teacher said⊙"The bus

will be ~~arriveing~~ **arriving** at 8⊙00 am." We ~~weighted~~ **waited** for

~~a~~ **an** hour, but no bus ~~never~~ showed up. We later

learned that the bus ~~breaked~~ **broke** down on ~~it's~~ **its** way

to our school. We ~~was~~ **were** all ~~vary~~ **very** disappointed.

**Unit 24 • Paragraph 96
Errors**

Capitalization 2
Colons 1
Commas. 1
Double
  Negatives. 1
Homophones 3
Periods. 1
Quotation
  Marks. 1
Spelling 1
Usage 1
Verbs 3

Total Errors: 15

Ralph aksed his little niece to name her

favorite book. She thinked about it for a long wile

and then said, My favorite book is The Cat in the

Hat by Dr seuss. Ralph nodded his head and said

"Thats a grate choice. I loved that book when I

was ur age."

Dr Jack R Jones and mr. ted Ames moved they

familys into the two new house up on the hill.

Both of their wifes love there new houses. Mr.

Jones house is a bit biger, but Mr. Ames house

has a nicer view

Ralph ~~aksed~~ *asked* his little niece to name her favorite book. She ~~thinked~~ *thought* about it for a long ~~wile~~ *while* and then said, "My favorite book is <u>The Cat in the Hat</u> by Dr. seuss." Ralph nodded his head and said, "Thats a ~~grate~~ *great* choice. I loved that book when I was ~~ur~~ *your* age."

Unit 25 • Paragraph 97
Errors

Apostrophes 1
Capitalization 1
Commas 1
Homophones 2
Periods 1
Quotation
  Marks 2
Spelling 2
Underlines 1
Verbs 1

Total Errors: 12

Dr. Jack R. Jones and mr. ted Ames moved ~~they~~ *their* ~~familys~~ *families* into the two new house*s* up on the hill. Both of their ~~wifes~~ *wives* love ~~there~~ *their* new houses. Mr. Jones*'s* house is a bit ~~biger~~ *bigger*, but Mr. Ames*'s* house has a nicer view.

Unit 25 • Paragraph 98
Errors

Apostrophes 2
Capitalization 2
Homophones 1
Periods 3
Plurals 3
Pronouns 1
Spelling 1

Total Errors: 13

Sams sister is taking six class at boston

University this Fall. Shes studying to be a writer

and a editor. She'd luv to write books for childs

one day. She tell Sam that her first book will

bee about a frendly frog named ribbit.

martins mom write storys for a magazine called

Mysteries Monthly. Her most recent peace of fiction

is called The Tree that Lost It's Leaves. Its about

a old tree that comes to life every Winter and

disappear into the forest

Sam's sister is taking six class*es* at boston

University this *F*all. She's studying to be a writer

and *an* a editor. She'd ~~luv~~ *love* to write books for ~~childs~~ *children*

one day. She tell*s* Sam that her first book will

be*e* about a fr*i*endly frog named ribbit.

Unit 25 • Paragraph 99
Errors

Apostrophes..... 2
Capitalization 3
Homophones 1
Plurals 2
Spelling 2
Usage 1
Verbs 1

Total Errors: 12

martins mom write*s* ~~storys~~ *stories* for a magazine called

Mysteries Monthly. Her most recent ~~peace~~ *piece* of fiction

is called "The Tree that Lost ~~It's~~ *Its* Leaves." It's about

an a old tree that comes to life every *w*inter and

disappear*s* into the forest.

Unit 25 • Paragraph 100
Errors

Apostrophes..... 2
Capitalization 2
Homophones 2
Periods......... 1
Plurals 1
Quotation
  Marks........ 2
Underlines 1
Usage 1
Verbs 2

Total Errors: 14

Editing Marks

Here is a list of the editing marks that are used in this book.

Mark	Meaning	Example
≡	Capitalize	We visited france.
/	Lowercase	It is Summer.
∧	Insert	We at tacos today.
ℊ	Delete	I likes that movie.
⊙	Add Period	I am here
?	Add Question Mark	Who is it
!	Add Exclamation Point	Watch out
Ⓘ	Add Comma	He lives in Ames Iowa.
⋮	Add Colon	I woke up at 630.
⌐	Add Apostrophe	That is Bobs hat.
" "	Add Quotation Marks	I said, See you soon."
___	Add Underline	I saw Star Wars twice.